The Great Coast Show

HILARY MOORCROFT and RICHARD OFFEN

THE NATIONAL TRUST

NEPTUNE COASTLINE CAMPAIGN

All Aboard!

Ever since its foundation in 1895 the National Trust has cared about the coastline. Since 1965 its coastal conservation project, the Neptune Coastline Campaign, has raised money to acquire and preserve fine coastal land and to alert people to the developments and pressures on the coast. Today the Trust safeguards 600 miles (965 km) of the coastal zone in England, Wales and Northern Ireland, while in Scotland a similar task is carried out by a separate organisation, the National Trust for Scotland.

To highlight the pressing conservation issues, the National Trust Coast Show is sailing around Britain during 2000. Aboard *Grand Turk*, a replica eighteenth-century tall ship, which starred as HM frigate *Indefatigable* in the television series of the popular *Hornblower* novels, the Neptune Coastline Campaign is raising funds to protect Britain's coastline and wildlife. And at each port of call, visitors will have the rare opportunity to catch a glimpse into the world of these wonderful vessels as *Grand Turk* prepares to set sail with the National Trust in defence of the British coast.

The first stroke of luck for the newly-founded National Trust was the gift of the small coastal property at Dinas Oleu, overlooking Barmouth in North Wales, to stop the development of the town and preserve it as a 'quiet place' to investigate and enjoy.

Ship Ahoy!

Horatio Hornblower is the creation of author C. S. Forester who published the first adventures of his intrepid hero in 1937, starting in Hornblower's mid-career when he was already captain of his own frigate. Realising the popularity of his character, Forester went on to write further stories of the inexperienced young midshipman, newly commissioned into Nelson's navy, and of the older officer making his way up the ladder of promotion to Admiral of the Fleet. Forester was a skilled amateur sailor with a detailed knowledge of the Navy and sailing ships of the eighteenth century. He completed ten novels and several short stories, and was working on a new adventure at the time of his death in 1966.

Hornblower owes much to the real-life characters of officers such as Lord Cochrane and Alexander Gordon, whose daring exploits on the high seas were documented in the naval chronicles and memoirs of the period. Throughout his career, Hornblower is a humble and insecure man who has a problem making friends. His love life has its ups and downs; he worries about his career and finances; he sweats that his honour will be lost. He is never convinced that he is a rival to Horatio Nelson, but his clever manoeuvres and quick thinking save the day time and again – much to the amazement of those around him. Hornblower thinks only that he has, once again, narrowly escaped total disaster… and thank heavens the Admiralty will never hear about this one!

At its height in the late eighteenth century, the British Navy operated over a thousand sailing ships. The largest vessels carried 120 guns, giving each ship as much fire power as a land army. These were 'ships of the line', which faced the enemy in a bow-to-stern or 'broadside' position. Frigates like *Grand Turk* were developed in the middle of the eighteenth century as three-masted ships, fully-rigged on each mast and armed with up to forty-four guns. They were smaller vessels and never fought in the line, but were fast and manoeuvrable, good for solo operations, and their commanders were admired for their tenacity and fine seamanship.

Children aboard *Grand Turk* as she prepares to set sail on her great adventure with the National Trust Coast Show.

Life afloat in Nelson's navy

The Royal Navy of Nelson's time fought almost every other nation in the world, defended Britain's colonial communications and trade, and landed troops in dozens of operations from Java to the West Indies. As Britain grew increasingly wealthy from overseas trade, she became ever more dependent on the free and safe use of the sea passages.

Naval officers began their training early. Admiral Lord Nelson went to sea at the age of twelve as a 'captain's servant' or cabin boy, and at twenty served as a midshipman before rising to the rank of post-captain at twenty-one. Midshipmen, who ensured that the captain's orders were carried out, earned only £22.50 a year, but the brightest recruits could look forward to a career as a commissioned officer earning between £100 and £400 per year. Although a naval academy had opened in Portsmouth in 1728 and a system of examinations had been introduced, it was possible for a cabin boy to rise through the ranks until 1859, when the *Britannia* became the training school for naval cadets.

There was nothing in the way of training or inducements for the sailors who, despite representing the lifeline of the nation, were notorious for being the dregs of society. In times of war, there was always a shortage of sailors and until 1815 the press gang was the accepted method of recruitment, with men being forcibly 'impressed' or seized in towns by the sea and taken aboard. Many must have been totally unfitted for life at sea; whilst untrained men could pull ropes, swab decks and manhandle guns, skilled hands were needed to work on the rigging as 'topmen' hanging up to 100 feet (over 30 metres) above the deck in howling wind or rain furling and unfurling sails.

There was no comfort below deck, which was dark, airless, damp and infested with rats and cockroaches. Disease could ravage a ship, and together with accidents claimed more lives than enemy action. The quality and variety of the food was not good: the meat was often bad and the bread full of weevils (beetles). The standard weekly ration was:

4 pounds of salt beef	2 pounds of salt pork
2 pints of pease (peas)	3 pints of oatmeal
6 ounces of butter	12 ounces of cheese

Rum – grog – had been issued as an official ration in the Royal Navy since the capture of Jamaica in 1655. There was also a daily allowance of bread and a gallon of beer. Fresh vegetables were issued when available and scurvy was defeated with the introduction to the seaman's diet of lime juice, lemons and, later, canned foods.

Ships' crews were highly organised. The best officers relied on strong leadership to make their ships efficient, but flogging and other punishments played an important part in naval discipline, as it did in law enforcement on land.

Lord George Graham in his Cabin painted in 1745 by William Hogarth. Lord Graham (1715–47) was the younger son of the Duke of Montrose. Like Hornblower, he began his naval career as a midshipman, rising to the rank of captain in 1740. He is shown dressed informally in a dressing-gown and turban for lunch with his purser; his wig is sported by Hogarth's pug. The picture hangs in the National Maritime Museum in Greenwich.

'The mart of many nations'

When the Romans arrived in Britain in the first century AD, they established a settlement on the Thames called Londinium from which they exported products such as skins, grain, hunting dogs, cattle, iron, tin and silver. These were exchanged for ivory, amber, glassware and pottery. Even after the Romans had left, the city continued to develop: the eighth-century monastic chronicler the Venerable Bede described London as the 'metropolis of the East Saxons' and 'the mart of many nations resorting to it by sea and land'.

The treasure trove unearthed at Sutton Hoo in Suffolk in 1939 has provided fascinating information about the wealth of Anglo-Saxon England – much of which indicates the importance of trade. The seventh-century ship-burial contained all the wealth and panoply of an Anglo-Saxon leader with objects in precious metals, textiles and wood gathered from all over the known world, from Scandinavia to Byzantium. The many lavish gold, bronze and jewelled items unearthed at Sutton Hoo can now be seen in the British

Museum, and the rest of the estate was given to the National Trust by the Annie Tranmer Charitable Trust in 1998. The main objective now is the long-term protection of the archaeological site, which comprises eighteen burial mounds and graves dating between the fifth and eleventh centuries. The Trust will leave these as untouched as possible, and a display centre will ensure public access and explain the history and significance of the site.

England's most prosperous export was wool, which was recognised as the finest raw material by the weavers of Flanders and Northern Italy. Wool and, later, cloth remained the main exports to Europe for hundreds of years.

Sutton Hoo in Suffolk. Although no body was discovered in the ship at Sutton Hoo, the Anglo-Saxons and the Vikings often buried important people in their ships so that they could sail to the land of the dead.

Wealth from wool

The modern ports of Ipswich in Suffolk and Hull in Yorkshire offer access to North West Europe and the North Sea shipping lanes, and trading links with Europe were established at both early in their history. They exported the produce of their hinterland, notably wool and cloth, and local merchants prospered.

The clothier Thomas Paycocke and his wife, Margaret, were among the beneficiaries of the East Anglian wool trade. Their house at Coggeshall in Essex was built in the early sixteenth century and was intended to impress. It was both their home and work place with a wide gateway entrance for wagons, an attic for storing wool and peg holes in the studs of the wall to hold the warp thread of the looms.

East Anglia was renowned for its worsteds, made from long wool that was prepared for spinning by combing, producing a smooth fine yarn and a lightweight cloth. From the mid-sixteenth century the region's cloth trade was boosted by the arrival of Huguenot and Flemish weavers who had fled from religious persecution. Their 'New Draperies', mixtures of silk and wool, were in great demand, and business boomed.

In Hull, the Industrial Revolution encouraged trade to thrive, and sailing ships would have created a delightful scene as they passed along channels close to the central streets of the town. As the port grew, so too did the fishing and whaling industries, producing two prized materials – whalebone, the plastic of the eighteenth century, and oil. Despite a decline in the fishing trade, Hull remains a major fishing port with vast docks and a large fleet of long-distance trawlers.

Paycocke's in Essex, built in the early sixteenth century for the clothier Thomas Paycocke and his wife. The intricate wood carvings on the beams of the half-timbered house proclaim the enhanced status of the wool merchant.

From coal to battleships

For centuries, sailing ships on Tyneside were agents of prosperity and change. The river communities traded in wool and hides, but from the mid-thirteenth century Newcastle developed as the first English coal-shipping port because of the neighbouring coalfields in Durham and Northumberland. The export of coal grew with particular demand from Flanders and Holland, which lacked timber for fuel, and coal rapidly became the Tyne's dominant cargo. A community of highly-skilled boatmen sprang up around the trade – the keelmen – who took their name from the small vessels that ferried the coal from the riverside to waiting ships.

At the end of the eighteenth century, large fleets of colliers – sometimes more than a hundred at a time – could be seen leaving the Tyne, taking the coal to London and elsewhere, and at the mouth of the river, North Shields Harbour was a scene of almost constant movement. Here, fish – cod and haddock – have been brought ashore for centuries: the name 'shiel' means fisherman's abode. The North Shields fleet fish throughout the North Sea and, although the fishing industry is now smaller and the fish not so bountiful, many families still earn their living from the sea.

With the Industrial Revolution, Newcastle became established as a mighty marine engineering centre, and in the late nineteenth century the river was alive to the sound of shipbuilding. The aircraft carrier *Ark Royal* was constructed at the Swan Hunter yard as late as 1981.

Many made their fortunes in the coal and shipping trades of Tyneside and the industries associated with them – among them was William Armstrong, the very model of Victorian enterprise and capitalism. He invented the first rifled gun and his plan for a hydraulic crane was adopted for the docks at Liverpool. His business expanded to include the construction of warships and at its peak around the end of the nineteenth century, Lord Armstrong's works employed 20,000 people. His Northumbrian country house at Cragside near Rothbury was as innovative as its owner, and was the first private house in the world to be completely lit by hydro-electricity, powered by a stream and reservoirs in the grounds.

The launch of HMS *Victoria*, a turret ship constructed by Lord Armstrong's firm, on the River Tyne in 1887.

Cleaning up the coal coast

When the Durham collieries were booming, five mines ran conveyor belts from their pitheads over the clifftops and dumped chunks of coal waste, rock, girders and abandoned iron buckets directly onto the sand. The beaches became blackened and despoiled, the creamy limestone cliffs were obscured and black sludge extended 300 feet (nearly 100 metres) into the North Sea. The mines provided thousands of jobs, and it was argued that miners' livelihoods would be sacrificed if the pits had to dump their waste elsewhere. But the collieries began to shut as mining became less profitable, and the British Coal Board had no further use for the beaches. After the mines had closed, local people collected coal from among the shale and shingle, and sold it for £2 a bag. But it was feared that the land would be sold on for further industrial use, with new owners continuing to use it as a dump.

Oliver Maurice, the National Trust's director of this region in the 1980s, looked beyond the scars and saw that much of the Durham coast was of merit with some of the finest cliffs in the country and the lovely steep-sided wooded valleys or denes running inland, providing habitats for rare butterflies and wild flowers. The Trust therefore began to acquire some of this land. First came Beacon Hill in 1987, and a year later the Trust paid British Coal £1 for a stretch of clifftop and beach near Horden Colliery at Warren House Gill, including part of Fox Holes Dene. It was the 500th mile of coast acquired under the Trust's Neptune campaign, and was celebrated as a great milestone, and as an indication of the faith that so many had come to place in the National Trust as a means of protecting our coastal heritage.

Today the Trust looks after 4½ miles (over 7 km) of Durham coast, and much has already been done to restore the area. The sea is undertaking most of the cleaning work – tidal action is slowly absorbing the sludge and clearing the coal waste to return the beaches to sand. The Trust is removing the eyesores that remain, and encourages local people to use the coastal footpaths and enjoy the landscape.

The magnesian limestone grassland along the cliffs is the habitat of the Durham Argus butterfly (*Arica artaxerxes*), which is found only on this part of the coast.

Hawthorne Hive in Durham in August 1998. The colliery waste spewed onto the rocky beach is still gradually eroding away more than ten years after the coal mines closed.

Guiding ships at night

England's oldest lighthouse is the Roman 'pharos' at Dover, which guided shipping in the Straits of Dover and in the first century AD sent signals across the Channel to its vanished partner in Boulogne. With the growth of seaborne trade the need for lighthouses grew, and in this country, Trinity House, set up in 1514 by Henry VIII, became responsible for lighthouses and other marks of the sea around the coast of England and Wales to guide mariners safely into port.

Early lighthouses were made of wood and lit by braziers in which coal or wood was burnt but were later replaced by oil lamps reflecting off mirrors. The first lighthouse to work in this way was set up on the banks of the Mersey by William Hutchinson, dockmaster at Liverpool in 1763. The first stone lighthouse was also built in the eighteenth century on the treacherous Eddystone Rocks 14 miles (22.5 km) off Plymouth. This lit the English Channel from 1759 until 1882 when it became unsafe and was replaced.

Today radio and satellite navigation systems have greatly reduced the need for large lighthouses. Most still in operation are automated; others are now redundant. The National Trust protects two of these: the South Foreland Lighthouse in Kent and Souter Lighthouse in South Tyneside, which opened in 1871 and was the first to be powered by alternating electric current.

Lighthouse keepers were often the first to notice ships in trouble: in 1838 Grace Darling and her father, the keeper of the Longstone lighthouse on the Farne Islands, heroically rescued passengers from the stricken steamer *Forfarshire*. The first self-righting lifeboat was built in the North East and launched on the River Tyne in 1789, and the world's first lifeboat service began here, saving hundreds of lives off the rocky Northumberland coast. The Royal National Lifeboat Institution, founded in 1824, has continued the work of bringing people to safety. Its fleet of lifeboats with their volunteer crews – on standby twenty-four hours a day – have saved 133,000 lives.

The sextant (above), which was used to measure distances, was one of the few navigational aids available on board ship in the eighteenth century.

The South Foreland Lighthouse in Kent was opened in 1843 to guide shipping through the ever-shifting banks of the Goodwin Sands to Dover.

Linking two seas

By 1600 Dundee was an important fishing port, busily engaged in North Sea trade and one of Scotland's largest whaling fleets also came to be based here. Whaling was a speculative, arduous and often dangerous trade in an age of sail with hand-held harpoons, but it proved highly profitable for shipowners prepared to take the risk. In the nineteenth century, as a by-product of this, Dundee's jute industry emerged after the discovery that raw jute imported from India could be woven into coarse fabrics when mixed with whale oil. The city became a world centre for jute-manufacturing, exporting more than ninety products including mats, bags, sacks, sailcloth and rope.

Before railways, goods were transported across the country by canal boats which travelled by inland routes and avoided the worst of the weather. The Caledonian Canal, which links a chain of lakes to connect the North Sea with the Irish Sea, is one of the most scenic. It was constructed between 1803 and 1822 by Thomas Telford, and is about 60 miles (100 km) long with 23 miles (37 km) of artificial channels. The great flight of eight locks at Banavie, known as 'Neptune's Staircase', is probably the most celebrated section.

A powder horn which may be seen aboard *Grand Turk*. Off-duty seamen on whaling ships often carved designs on whales' teeth or walrus tusks. It became known as scrimshaw, perhaps after Admiral Scrimshaw who was said to be an exponent of the art.

The Caledonian Canal, a haven for pleasure boats since the advent of ocean-going steamships, which were too large to sail down its channels.

Defending the realm

The earliest English ship known to have carried guns was the *Christine*, which was armed with three iron guns and a handgun, and was captured by the French in 1340 at the Battle of Sluys. The *Christine of the Tower*, built in 1406 is traditionally said to be the first English ship in which guns were properly mounted. Early naval cannon were spectacularly inaccurate, and as likely to kill the men who fired them as kill the enemy.

The one-street village of Smallhythe in Kent once boasted a busy shipyard and quays on the tidal River Rother. This is almost impossible to imagine today: it is now 8 miles (13 km) from the sea! But during the reign of Henry VIII, important warships were built there for the royal fleet, and the king came personally to inspect their progress.

Henry VIII was ardently interested in ships and set out to create a significant navy. For much of his reign, England was at war with France, so it was essential to equip ships with heavy cannon to attack the French coastline and shipping. Dockyards were built on the Thames at Woolwich and Deptford – both conveniently close to the Royal Palace at Greenwich. Shipwright to the king was James Baker, inventor of the 'broadside' tactic. This was a turning point in the history of naval warfare, as the means of attack moved from the 'fighting castle' to the side of the ship, and enemy vessels could be sunk from considerable distances. One of the earliest ships designed to fight in this way was the galleon *Mary Rose*,

Henry VIII's favourite ship, which was named after his sister. Unfortunately in 1545, after thirty-four years' service in Henry's navy, *Mary Rose* sank off Portsmouth. Her hull was discovered by divers four hundred years later.

Control of the sea was particularly important for Britain during the Napoleonic Wars. Martello towers – circular forts – were hastily erected along the south and east coasts to guard against invasion, but it was felt that it was only a matter of time before Napoleon attempted to cross the Channel. The most likely place for the French to land was believed to be Dungeness in Kent, which would be difficult to defend because it was mainly marshland. It was therefore decided to build a canal as a defence that could also transport troops and ammunition. But by the time the Royal Military Canal had been built, the French had lost the Battle of Trafalgar in 1805 and turned their attention to war on land, leaving the British high command with embarrassing questions about the appallingly high cost of a '30-mile ditch' which did nothing and went nowhere. Today $3^{1}/_{2}$ miles (5.5 km) of the canal, between Warehorne and Appledore are in the care of the National Trust and open to walkers.

In the fifteenth century Smallhythe Place in Kent was better known as the Port House, where the harbour-master lived. The retreat of the sea has left it high and dry, and the house is now preserved by the National Trust as a theatrical museum – a tribute to its most famous owner, the actress Ellen Terry.

Turk – a Thames tradition

Board a Turk's boat and you experience part of an unbroken tradition of boat-building and passenger boat operation on the Thames, stretching back to the time of Richard the Lionheart. Early records show the Turk family engaged in building two galleys for 'the defence of the Realm' on land near the Tower of London in 1195, and a shipwright named Turk was Lord Mayor of London in 1230, long before Dick Whittington made his famous journey.

The modern business was established by Richard Turk in Kingston upon Thames, Surrey, in 1710 during the reign of Queen Anne, when road transport was still both difficult and dangerous and the river ruled. Today R. J. Turk & Sons and its associated companies are run by Richard's great-great-great grandson, Michael, who intends to keep them in the family.

Initially, the firm concentrated on building passenger wherries and fishing punts, but its reputation spread and soon it was making boats for English and foreign royalty and exporting pleasure craft – especially canoes and skiffs – all over the world, often winning prizes at international exhibitions. Turks even built boats for the amusement of Queen Victoria on the Home Park waters at Windsor Castle in Berkshire.

Grand Turk is the result of Michael Turk's life-long ambition to build and operate a representative vessel of the Nelson era. She was built in Marmaris, Turkey, from mahogany and iroko (a Burmese teak that is relatively insect-proof), but her masts are solid tree trunks grown in the Forest of Dean in Gloucestershire. Launched in 1997, the 20-cannon *Grand Turk* is 152 feet (46.3 metres) long with a mainmast 117 feet (35.7 metres) above the water. Her rigging contains more than 3 miles (nearly 5 km) of rope, and she can travel at up to 10 knots under sail.

Diagram of *Grand Turk*, which was modelled on the eighteenth-century frigate HM *Blandford*.

- Foremast
- Mainmast
- Top gallant
- Topsail yard
- Fighting Top
- Course yard
- Mizenmast
- Fighting Top
- FOREDECK
- Catshead
- Mizen topmast staysail
- Mizen course
- Spanker
- MAIN DECK
- POOP DECK

A place 'worth seeing'

Belfast gained importance as the market centre for the Ulster linen industry, which was developed by French Huguenot refugees. The town was a busy port with small shipbuilding interests, which became firmly established after William Ritchie founded a shipyard in 1791 and soon afterwards a graving (dry) dock. Many of the world's largest steamers were built in Belfast – including the ill-fated *Titanic*.

Coastline of magnificent beauty, much of it protected by the National Trust, is within a short distance of Belfast. To the north, the spectacular scenery of the Antrim coast is remarkable for the richness of its flora and fauna: on the cliffs at Downhill, the dunes of Portstewart Strand, the chalk bastions of sweeping Whitepark Bay and the basalt walls of Fair Head. Best known is the Giant's Causeway, an extraordinary collection of some 40,000 basalt columns formed by volcanic activity. Legend has it that the causeway was built by the giant, Finn MacCool (mac Cumhaill), who intended either to fight another giant or to meet his lady friend: you can take your pick!

South of Belfast, Strangford Lough is one of the largest sea inlets in the British Isles and extremely rich in maritime wildlife – more than 2,000 different species are found here, ranging from common and grey seals to sea cucumber, curled octopus and dog cockles.

The Giant's Causeway in County Antrim, which, according to Dr Johnson, was 'worth seeing, but not worth going to see'. Today the causeway attracts over half a million visitors each year who would probably disagree.

Rivals on the westward trading route

Whitehaven in Cumbria was an early coal-mining centre with some of the mines running several miles under the sea. As early as the twelfth century coal and building stones were shipped from the port; stone for the building of St George's Chapel at Windsor Castle came from here. The coal port grew rapidly in the eighteenth century, and a trade based on exporting manufactured goods to America and the West Indies and importing tobacco, sugar and other colonial goods brought great wealth to Whitehaven.

Whitehaven's status made her a legitimate target during the American War of Independence. As Commander of the *Ranger*, Scottish-born John Paul Jones was ordered to cruise the British Isles to 'distress' the enemy. In 1778 he attacked Whitehaven, set fire to one ship and spiked the battery guns, but failed to capture the town. Jones went on to command the *Bonhomme Richard* and win America's first major victory, the Battle of Flamborough Head in 1779.

In the nineteenth century Liverpool began to take markets away from Whitehaven and became the port for Lancashire's developing industries – cotton and glass manufacturing. The Mersey teemed with ships: Liverpool's seaborne commerce encompassed the world, and in 1840 the Cunard Company incorporated a regular passenger service to New York.

At the end of the eighteenth century Liverpool had also become a centre for the slave trade. The process was triangular: ships would be laden with goods to barter with West African chiefs in exchange for a human cargo, and then sailed to the West Indies or America. Here captives were sold to work in the sugar and cotton plantations. A return cargo of sugar, rum, cotton or tobacco was purchased with the proceeds and the ship sailed back to England. Wealthy local merchant Richard Watt, for example, made his fortune in the West Indies and lived in the fine Tudor mansion of Speke Hall. His godson, Richard Watt III was the chief beneficiary of his will, which included a plantation in Jamaica together with 'the Negroes and other slaves'. Slavery was abolished in the British Empire in 1833, and in the USA in 1865, after the Civil War.

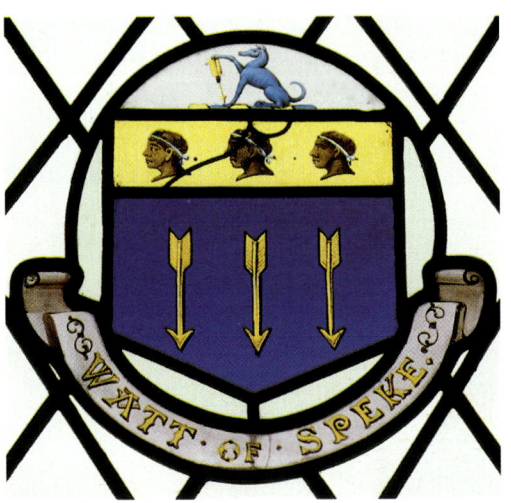

The three blackamoor heads in Richard Watt's coat of arms (above), which can be seen in stained glass at Speke Hall, acknowledge the origin of his wealth in the Jamaican sugar plantations.

Today Liverpool's Albert Dock is home to a branch of the Tate Gallery and Merseyside Maritime Museum which explains the city's seafaring history. In the nineteenth century this was 'the Port of a Thousand Ships' with some of the earliest steamships leaving to make the Atlantic crossing, and clippers sailing to China, India and Australia.

The shifting sands of time

Just 10 miles (16 km) north of Liverpool city centre, the beleaguered red squirrel is alive and well at Formby. Across England and Wales, the native British squirrel has become sadly scarce

following the invasion of their habitats by the grey squirrel, which was introduced from America at the end of the nineteenth century and multiplied at an amazing rate. At Formby, and on Brownsea Island in Poole Harbour, Dorset, the National Trust ensures that these beautiful creatures are protected from the advance of the greys.

More rarely seen by the visitor, the natterjack toad is another endangered species, which lives on sand dunes, heaths and saltmarshes. This mainly nocturnal creature can be identified by the yellow stripes down its back and, to encourage its successful breeding at Formby, artificial toad scrapes or freshwater pools have been dug where it can find the right conditions for spawning and growth of its tadpoles.

Ancient human footprint trails are also sometimes found at Formby, exposed in clay layers that are uncovered by the sea eroding the coastline. The people who made these prints must have spent quite a lot of time on the beach, perhaps collecting food or driftwood. Other prints include extinct birds and mammals, and hoof-prints of deer may indicate early farming and animal husbandry. Appearing under certain tidal conditions, the prints are tantalisingly ephemeral as they are soon washed away.

The forces of wind and tide, causing accretion and erosion, continuously alter the shape of the Formby coastline. The town today is separated from the sea by more than a mile (nearly 2 km) of high sand dunes which built up over the centuries, but measurements taken since 1906 reveal that nearly $1/4$ mile (400 metres) has been lost in places by wave erosion. Thus the natural cycle continues, and so do man's efforts to control it. The main technique, as it was 250 years ago, is to introduce marram grass. This is planted to arrest the drifting sand, binding it with tangled roots and preventing the wind from blowing the sand away.

A glorious expanse of rippled sands at Formby Point, Merseyside. The pine woods on the hinterland help to control erosion – and support the red squirrel.

Speeding along the Welsh coast

In 1826 the Trustees of Liverpool Docks established a chain of semaphore signalling stations about 10 miles (16 km) apart along the coast from Liverpool to Holyhead for the purpose of reporting weather conditions and to enable shipowners to obtain news of the arrival of their vessels. The speed of the system was tested in 1830, when a question was sent from Liverpool to Holyhead, and the reply was received in just twenty-three seconds.

Holyhead has for so long been established as the road and rail terminus for ferries to Ireland that it may be difficult to imagine that the tranquil little harbour of Porthdinllaen on the Llŷn Peninsula, was once its main rival. Porthdinllaen was a small, flourishing seaside community and one of the most important herring fishing ports in North Wales with a thriving ship building industry. In 1819 a Parliamentary bill to make Porthdinllaen the packet port for Ireland failed to find enough support, and Holyhead was chosen instead – by just one vote. It is still darkly maintained that the geological samples that clinched the decision actually came from Porthdinllaen....

Rivalry flared again in 1837 with the arrival of the railways, and once more Holyhead gained the advantage with the building of the Chester-to-Holyhead railway. Porthdinllaen formed its own railway company in 1844, but the line was never built and the village's hope of becoming a major port vanished. Porthdinllaen was allowed to remain as a tiny settlement with a pub, a handful of cottages and the *Hettie Rampton*, a lifeboat with a notable service record.

The remote harbour of Porthdinllaen in Wales would have been a bustling port if its supporters had had their way in the nineteenth century. Since 1994 the entire headland has been in the care of the National Trust to ensure that the threat of port development will never occur again.

Jewels in a Welsh crown

Thanks to the Neptune Coastline Campaign, the National Trust protects about 50 miles (80 km) of rugged cliffs, dramatic headlands and sandy bays in Pembrokeshire. It is excellent for wildlife, with ravens, chough and grey seals to be seen. The Trust's coastal areas stretch from Dinas Island, 5 miles (8 km) east of Fishguard, to the Colby Estate in the south, passing St David's Head, Solva, the varied landscape of the Stackpole Estate and also 15½ miles (25 km) of coastline on St Bride's Bay, including the former deer park at Marloes and the tiny harbour of Martin's Haven.

In 1797, in the wake of the French Revolution, a party of Frenchmen landed at Carragwastad Point, north-west of Fishguard, but quickly gave themselves up. It is said that their surrender was hastened by the appearance of a large number of local women in red cloaks, armed with pitchforks, who were mistaken for soldiers!

Britain has never been invaded since.

The deep water inlet of Milford Haven was regarded by Nelson as one of the finest sheltered harbours in the world when he visited the town in 1802. Milford had been founded a few years earlier on land owned by Sir William Hamilton whose wife Emma became Nelson's mistress. Famous in the great days of the fishing industry, the Haven now handles large oil cargoes with sometimes devastating results. In 1996 the *Sea Empress* oil spill caused havoc, taking a heavy toll of seabirds which are highly vulnerable to oil pollution as they feed on or under the sea's surface. Many beaches were disaster areas, and handling the crisis took months out of the working life of local National Trust head warden Richard Ellis.

The Stackpole Estate boasts dizzying cliffs, beaches, a series of landlocked freshwater lakes, and the Quay, which originally served a limestone quarry. A host of sea creatures and plants may be found in the rock pools which form at low tide.

Smoke and iron from the valleys

At the beginning of the nineteenth century, the series of narrow valleys running down South Wales from the edge of the Brecon Beacons was wild country, containing few people, isolated farms and just a few small villages. By the end of the century, the valleys had become massively industrialised with pitheads, iron workings and long rows of terraced miners' houses stretching into the dusty mist.

Vast quantities of coal from the valleys kept the greatest navy in the world afloat and

powered the merchant ships with which Britain was building her empire. Coal was also used in the production of iron, which in turn spawned factory machinery, the cannons for the Napoleonic Wars, the first iron ships, and the railways, which opened up the American West. New technology in the nineteenth century enabled sheet iron to be rolled instead of hammered flat – the secret of canning. The huge increase in the use of canned food resulted in demands for Welsh tinplate from every part of the globe.

In the 1830s, South Wales began to develop its coal export industry. Deep inlets along the coast close to the rich coal seams made it even easier for coal to be transported. The pits thrust deeper and deeper – for the miners the work got harder and more dangerous – and the whole area became one of the most industrialised in the world.

Presiding over all this, the link between the booming Welsh industry and the sea, was the city of Cardiff. Vast fortunes were made in Cardiff's docklands, largely by the Crichton-Stuart family. They invested in the town's first dock which opened in 1839 and was linked by rail to the pitheads and ironworks, and John Patrick, 3rd Marquis of Bute, poured much of his wealth into the re-creation of Cardiff Castle, turning it into a Victorian fairytale palace.

Elsewhere, all along the coast, intruding on its natural beauty, burgeoning towns ran from Penarth, with its palatial homes of coalowners and shipping magnates, past the developing beaches and through to Port Talbot and Llanelli which became the centre of the tinplate industry. By the middle of the nineteenth century Newport also had a thriving dock and saw a huge industrial boom, and more than 10,000 ships sailed in and out of the port at Swansea.

In the 1790s a single warship could carry more than a hundred heavy guns which were frequently the product of Welsh iron. *Grand Turk* carries a modest twenty gunports and ammunition.

The struggle against Napoleon

In 1789 the French Revolution swept Louis XVI and his aristocrats from power. Out of the turmoil Napoleon Bonaparte emerged with a scheme for world domination: French armies marched into Belgium and Germany, and from 1793 Napoleon set his sights on invading Britain. He was so confident of success that proclamations dated from London were printed ready to distribute as soon as the French army reached the capital.

Napoleon intended that Admiral Pierre de Villeneuve should put out to sea from Toulon, lure Nelson's fleet into the Atlantic and then – having given him the slip – return to join the rest of the French fleet, which lay in harbour at Brest under Admiral Ganteaume. Immediately afterwards the invasion would begin. With the British navy out of the way searching the seas for the French ships, Bonaparte's army would be able cross the Channel unopposed.

In the spring of 1805 the decoy duly set off towards the West Indies with the British in pursuit. The French fleet doubled back, but were sighted in the Bay of Biscay by Sir Robert Calder who captured two ships and drove the rest to seek shelter in the harbour of Cádiz, causing Villeneuve to miss the rendezvous with Ganteaume. Instead, on venturing from Cádiz, he joined up with the Spanish fleet. The Combined Fleet sailed for the Channel but were sighted by the British fleet, under Admiral Nelson's command.

The Battle of Trafalgar was fought on 21 October 1805 off Cape Trafalgar between Cádiz and the Straits of Gibraltar. Before the battle, Nelson hoisted on his flagship the famous signal, 'England expects that every man will do his duty'. The battle raged at its fiercest around his ship *Victory*, and Nelson was struck by a bullet, but lived long enough to know that the battle was won.

Grand Turk a.k.a. *Indefatigable* (right) opens fire in the broadside position during the filming of *Hornblower*.

[36]

The finest natural harbour in the English Channel

In 1539 the Holy Roman Emperor Charles V and the French king, François I, threatened to combine to reclaim England for the Roman Catholic faith. Henry VIII was rightly alarmed at the thought of these two rivals getting together, and erected a series of castles along the south coast – the first true military fortifications to be built for many years. In Cornwall St Mawes and Pendennis were constructed on either side of Falmouth harbour, with a chain across to prevent entry to the deep water channel of Carrick Roads.

In the eighteenth century Falmouth was the port from which the packet ships carried mail overseas, while the letters they brought were despatched by road to London and other cities. The 'Falmouth packets' were fast, lightly-armed sailing vessels built locally and privately owned, under charter to the Post Office. Their mission involved them in numerous gun battles during the Napoleonic Wars – if capture was inevitable the mail was jettisoned overboard. By the early nineteenth century, as many as forty packets were operating out of Falmouth but, in the 1850s, with the coming of the railways and the steamship, the packet trade was lost to Southampton and Liverpool.

Falmouth was the first port of call for many ships homeward-bound and the last stopping place for those sailing west. The deep, sheltered waters of Carrick Roads were a safe refuge from storms and a convenient anchorage for vessels awaiting orders or replenishing their supplies. Falmouth's importance as a link with the outside world is emphasised by the fact that it was the first place in Britain to learn of Nelson's victory at Trafalgar. And today, in spite of the huge oil tankers and modern cargo ships using the port, Falmouth is still evocative of centuries of sail – from the Elizabethan galleons to the last of the great square-rigged clippers setting sail for Australia for their annual cargoes of grain.

The winding character of the Fal is a result of it being a drowned river valley, which was submerged by a rapid rise in sea level after the last ice age. At the head of the estuary, almost an island between two creeks, the wooded estate of Trelissick provides beautiful views of the Fal water-world. Trelissick was given to the National Trust in 1955 and the garden is open to visitors throughout the year. Much of the landscaping was done early in the nineteenth century by Ralph Allen Daniell, whose father, Thomas 'Guinea-a-Minute' Daniell had made his fortune from tin and copper mining in Cornwall.

Across Falmouth Bay in the densely-wooded upper reaches of the Helford River, the Trust looks after land at Penarvon Cove and Frenchman's Creek, made famous by Daphne du Maurier's tale of piracy and smuggling – it is easy enough to imagine smugglers coming into the inlet under cover of darkness. It may be that 'Frenchman' here means 'ship' in the sense that you find India*man* or *man* o' war and might be derived from an incident in the creek involving a French ship.

View towards St Mawes and the deep water channel of Carrick Roads from St Antony's Head in Cornwall. The castle on the cliff was built by Henry VIII as part of the defences against the French in the 1540s.

Tin and pilchards

The role of the National Trust in protecting unspoilt stretches of coastal land is clearly seen in Cornwall where the charity looks after more than a third of the total length of coastline. The Trust's involvement began in 1897 when Barras Nose, the headland north of Tintagel Castle, was bought to prevent the building of a hotel. Since then, the Trust has gone steadily forward, concentrating on acquiring unspoiled stretches where the land was threatened by development for the tourist trade. The policy of buying coastal land 'one farm deep' or 'to the skyline' in order to preserve the whole coastal landscape was initiated by Michael Trinick, the Trust's director for this region in the 1970s, whose energy and enthusiasm earned him the nickname 'King Neptune'.

In recent years, a number of important acquisitions have prevented more areas of Cornwall's most westerly landscape – West Penwith – from being despoiled. The prosperity of this area in former times was based on the summer pilchard shoals, the farming of the land and the mining of tin. Such was Cornwall's importance in the tin trade that in the mid-nineteenth century twelve countries had vice-consuls based in Penzance!

The ruins of engine houses scattered throughout West Penwith are a reminder of the days when fortunes were made in tin and copper mining. For centuries, deep mines were impossible because of flooding, and it was not until the eighteenth century that Thomas Newcomen invented a steam engine that would pump water from the workings. This was developed by the local engineer Richard Trevithick to become the Cornish beam engine which enabled mines to go down over 3,000 feet (900 metres) and stretch in narrow tunnels far under the sea. For more information about Cornwall's tin mines, visit the Count House at Botallack near St Just, which was the nineteenth-century office of the Botallack Mine, and has recently been restored by the National Trust.

The ruined pumping-engine house of the Levant Mine, which went over a mile (1.5 km) beneath the Atlantic. The pumps that drained the mines were housed in these buildings.

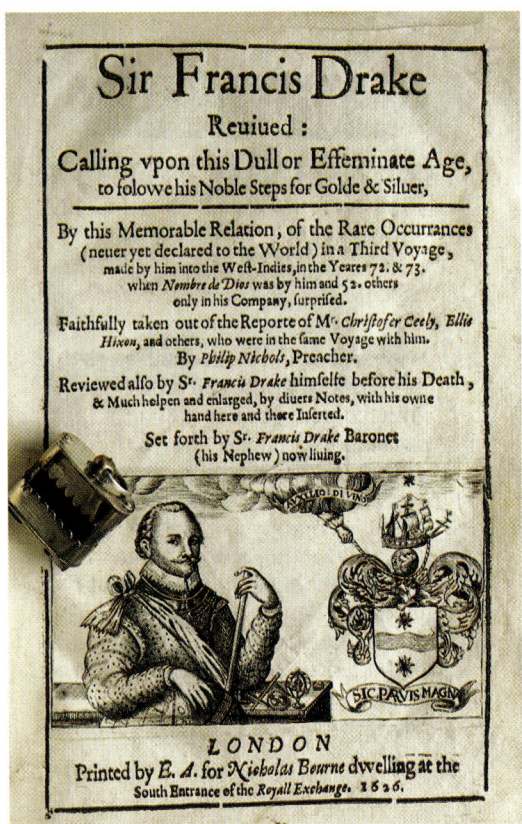

Buckland Abbey in Devon became the home of Sir Francis Drake on his return from sailing around the world. The house contains memorabilia from Drake's time including his lodestone and a memoir of his exploits (above).

Plymouth ho!

During the Hundred Years' War, many ships sailed from Plymouth to fight against France, and later it was the port from which the Elizabethan sailors John Hawkins, Walter Ralegh and Martin Frobisher embarked on their great voyages. Above all, it is the city of daredevil Francis Drake, the first Englishman to circumnavigate the world in the *Golden Hind*. Always a thorn in the flesh to the Spanish, Drake is said to have finished his game of bowls on the Hoe in 1588 before sailing out to destroy the Armada – aided by severe gales. The bowls are possible, but whether he actually said, 'We have time enough to finish the game and beat the Spaniards' is more doubtful: it was forty years before the remark was recorded!

In 1620 the *Mayflower* carried the Pilgrim Fathers from Plymouth to the New World in search of a place where they could worship as they wished. The square-rigged, double-decked vessel reached the Massachusetts coast of America after more than sixty days at sea, and the Puritans named their first settlement Plymouth. Thousands soon followed them and settled in the area that they called New England. In America Thanksgiving Day is a national holiday in memory of the gathering of the harvest by the Pilgrims at the end of their first year in the New World.

Captain James Cook also departed from Plymouth, in 1768, in command of HMS *Endeavour Bark* to carry out a voyage of scientific and geographical discovery in the vast, uncharted Pacific Ocean. Eight months later he landed on the island of Tahiti. In his three-year circumnavigation of the world, Cook learned to make very accurate maps and provided a wealth of new information, which paved the way for the settlement of Australia and New Zealand.

Much of the coastline around Plymouth has been built up in recent years, to cater for the growth of tourism. But some parts remain rural and unspoilt, and many of these are protected by the National Trust – like Pencarrow Head on the west bank of the River Tamar, an anonymous gift from a lover of Cornwall in 1959, and to the east both banks of the beautiful Yealm estuary.

Watch the wall, my darling

> Five and twenty ponies,
> Trotting through the dark –
> Brandy for the Parson,
> 'Baccy for the Clerk;
> Laces for a lady; letters for a spy,
> And watch the wall, my darling,
> while the Gentlemen go by!

Rudyard Kipling's romantic chorus to *A Smugglers' Song* perfectly captures the climate that supported a huge trade in illegal imports during the eighteenth and early nineteenth centuries.

During the eighteenth century, the trade in contraband across Britain's coasts expanded at such a rate that the excise men could not keep up. A trade that had existed as simple, small-scale evasion of duty had become an industry of astonishing proportions, channelling volumes of goods such as brandy, gin (known as *geneva*), rum, lace, gloves, jewellery and, in huge quantities, tea into the southern counties of England. At one stage it was reckoned that more spirits were coming through Devon and Cornwall illicitly than were entering the country legally through the London docks!

Romney Marsh in Kent was one of the main centres for smuggling in the south east. The area was reclaimed from the sea by the Romans and has a mystique of its own. As the Reverend Richard Harris Barham, the author of a collection of poems called *The Ingoldsby Legends*, claimed in 1877:

> The World is divided into five parts,
>   namely Europe,
> Asia, Africa, America and Romney Marsh.

Barham was Rector of Snargate, one of the marshland's lonely churches, and allowed smugglers to use it to store contraband – it was said you could find your way directly to his church by the aroma of tobacco!

Over the centuries, many ships have foundered off the treacherous coasts of Devon and Cornwall, and stories abound of how local people have ransacked vessels that have been smashed to pieces on the rocks. In Portlemouth, Devon, a story is told of how a particularly dry and tedious sermon was interrupted one Sunday morning. A man entered the church, admitting the howling gale without, and whispered in the vicar's ear. The congregation was immediately roused from its slumbers when the vicar bellowed, 'There's a ship ashore between Prawle and Pear Tree Point!' The clergyman quickly disrobed, and the congregation rose and charged headlong to the beach, with the vicar at their head. The legend goes on to relate that the parishioners ignored the cries of the drowning crew as they tried to salvage cargo from the galleon.

Smugglers, a watercolour by J. A. Atkinson *c.*1808. As they unloaded their goods, smugglers kept a careful look out for the Revenue Cutters or the Coastguard. Informers would be rewarded by the authorities if they were caught red-handed with the contraband.

Gateway to England

The strategic position of Dover in Kent, just 20 miles (32 km) from the coast of France, has been recognised since Roman times; the tallest surviving Roman structure in Britain is the 'pharos' lighthouse, built on the highest point of an Iron Age fort. Later, soon after the Battle of Hastings in 1066, the Normans built a castle next to the site and such was its importance that it was garrisoned through to 1958. It was not the most comfortable place in the world: in 1753 General James Wolfe spent the winter at Dover Castle with six companies of the 20th Regiment of Foot. 'I lodge at the foot of a tower supposed to be built by the Romans,' he wrote gloomily to his mother, 'and cannot help wishing sometimes that they had chosen a snugger situation.'

Dover Castle is now looked after by English Heritage, and visitors can learn about its key role in defending the country from invasion over the centuries. In 1216 the castle was besieged by French troops under Prince Louis. The English tunnelled through the chalk so that the soldiers could re-group at the northern outworks and attack. The tunnels were extended 600 years later when Napoleon threatened to invade; in 1940 they became the headquarters from which Admiral Ramsay directed Operation Dynamo – the evacuation of allied soldiers from Dunkirk.

The famous White Cliffs may be enjoyed from above: the National Trust protects over 5 miles (8 km) from Great Farthingloe stretching east to Langdown Cliffs and St Margaret's Bay, where the South Foreland Lighthouse (see p.17) stands proud. The chalk downland is grazed by Exmoor ponies and sheep, and wild flowers abound, including pyramidal and bee orchids. Kittiwakes breed here, and migrant birds mimic their human counterparts as they too arrive and depart from the White Cliffs.

The White Cliffs of Dover provide the first glimpse of England to the traveller crossing the Channel and speed the parting guest.

Places to visit and useful addresses

National Trust Properties

The National Trust looks after historic houses and gardens throughout England, Wales and Northern Ireland – for more information consult the National Trust *Handbook* (price £4.50 – free to members) or visit our website at www.nationaltrust.org.uk. The National Trust *Coast and Countryside Handbook* (£7.99) also provides a host of ideas for days out at over 400 countryside properties.

If you would like to become a member and help the National Trust in its conservation work, please contact the Membership Department at The National Trust, PO Box 39, Bromley, Kent BR1 3XL, Tel: 020 8315 1111 e-mail: enquiries@ntrust.org.uk, who will be happy to help you. One of the benefits of membership is free entry into all National Trust properties, and those of the National Trust for Scotland.

For more information about properties in the care of the National Trust for Scotland, the *Guide to Properties of the National Trust for Scotland* is available from The National Trust for Scotland, Public Affairs Department, 28 Charlotte Square, Edinburgh EH2 4ET (£2.50 including post and packing), or from all NTS properties (price £2.00).

National Maritime Museum
Romney Road, Greenwich, London SE10 9NF (020 8858 4422)
The largest museum of its kind in the world, with over two million items in its collections. The museum also includes the Queen's House and the Royal Observatory, Greenwich.

Hull Maritime Museum
Queen Victoria Square, Hull HU1 3DX (01482 613 902)
Charts the history of the fishing and whaling industry in this country and houses an important collection of scrimshaw work.

Merseyside Maritime Museum
Albert Dock, Liverpool L3 4AQ (0151 207 0001)
Boasts a superb collection of model ships as well as fascinating galleries charting the history of emigration and slavery.

Flagship Portsmouth
HM Naval Base, Portsmouth PO1 3LJ (01705 861 512)
Home of the *Mary Rose*, HMS *Victory* and HMS *Warrior* as well as the Royal Naval Museum.

Cutty Sark
King William Walk, Greenwich, London SE10 9HT (020 8858 2698)
The world's sole surviving tea clipper, built in 1869.

HMS *Discovery*
Discovery Point, Discovery Quay, Dundee DD2 5BT (01382 201 245)
Research ship built for the 1901–4 Antarctic expedition. A quayside centre tells the story of the ship and polar exploration.

Royal National Lifeboat Institution Headquarters
West Quay Road, Poole, Dorset BH15 1HZ (01202 663 000)
The collection illustrates the history of the RNLI.

Grace Darling Museum
Radcliffe Road, Bamburgh, Northumberland NE69 7AE (01668 214 465)
One of many RNLI museums around the British Isles, the collection includes mementoes of the heroine Grace Darling.

Bamburgh Castle
Bamburgh, Northumberland NE69 7DF (01668 214 515)
Norman stronghold restored in the late nineteenth century by Lord Armstrong. The Farne Islands (NT), one of Britain's most important seabird sanctuaries, are just offshore (tel: 01665 721 099 for information).

Cardiff Castle
Castle Street, Cardiff CF10 3RB (02920 878 100)
Spectacular nineteenth-century Gothic interiors.

Dover Castle
Dover, Kent (01304 211 067)
Commanding the shortest sea crossing between England and the continent, Dover Castle has been a vital strategic centre since the Iron Age.

Time Tunnel
Lagan Lookout, 1 Donegall Quay, Belfast BT1 3EA (02890 315 444)
Illustrates the history of Belfast from the twelfth century to the present day.